The New Novello Choral Edition

FELIX MENDELSSOHN

Hymn of Praise
Lobgesang
Op. 52

for two soprano and tenor soloists, SATB and orchestra

English text by J. Alfred Novello after the Lutheran Bible

Vocal score

Revised by Michael Pilkington

Order No: NOV072506

NOVELLO PUBLISHING LIMITED

Orchestral material is available on hire from the Publisher.

It is requested that on all concert notices and programmes acknowledgement is made to 'The New Novello Choral Edition'.

Permission to reproduce from the Preface of this Edition must be obtained from the Publisher.

Cover illustration: first page of the final chorus from the autograph score of Mendelssohn's *Lobgesang* (courtesy of the Bibliotheka Jagiellońska, Cracow).

© 2001 Novello & Company Limited
Published in Great Britain by Novello Publishing Limited – Head Office: 14-15 Berners Street, LONDON W1D 3LJ
Tel +44 (0)20 7612 7400   Fax +44 (0)20 7612 7546

Sales and Hire: Music Sales Distribution Centre – Newmarket Road, Bury St Edmunds, Suffolk IP33 3YB
Tel +44 (0)1284 702600   Fax +44 (0)1284 768301
Web: www.musicsales.com   e-mail: music@musicsales.co.uk
All rights reserved   Printed in Great Britain
Music setting by Stave Origination

PREFACE

Hymn of Praise (Lobgesang) was composed in 1840 to celebrate the four-hundredth anniversary of the invention of printing. It seems probable that the orchestral piece which opens the work (not included in this vocal score) had already been planned before the commission arrived and that the cantata was then added. The words were taken from Luther's translation of the Old Testament[1]; having chosen them, Mendelssohn added at the top of his score: 'Sondern ich wöllt alle Künste, sonderlich die Musica, gern sehen im Dienst des der sie geben und geschaffen hat. - Dr M Luther.' (I would gladly see all the arts, especially music, serving him who has given them and made them what they are).

The first performance was in Leipzig on 25 June 1840, and a performance in Birmingham was planned for 23 September. On 21 July Mendelssohn wrote to the Birmingham Festival Manager, in English: 'I have found an Englishman here who translates the words for me. I preferred this, because I can always tell which parts I am able to alter, and which not; and if the task is done I shall send it to my friends in England to look over and alter it as they like.' However, Mendelssohn then fell ill. Worried that the English version for the Birmingham performance might be delayed, Alfred Novello went to Leipzig himself. 'Mr Novello settled the English text with Mendelssohn, and in three days started back to London'.[2]

As was later the case with *Elijah*, Mendelssohn was dissatisfied with his music and made considerable revisions to the work, adding Nos. 3, 6 and 9 to the cantata and providing a fully written out organ part for Nos. 2, 7, 8 and 10. In 1841, Breitkopf & Härtel published the full score, in German and English, while Novello published a very handsome vocal score, English only, at the unusually high price of one guinea. In spite of the disagreements shown in the English text, Breitkopf & Härtel mention Novello on the title page, and Novello include the name Breitkopf & Härtel. In 1846, Novello started the 'Octavo' editions of choral works and, in 1857, issued *Hymn of Praise* in the series, with both German and English words. In 1875 Breitkopf & Härtel issued a new full score as part of the Complete Works series, German only, edited by Julius Rietz. Perhaps in reply, in about 1890, Novello published a full score for the first time, handsomely produced but English only.

The English text raises some problems. Alfred Novello was only in Leipzig for three days, and though he may have 'settled the English text with Mendelssohn', he would hardly have had time to fit the words of the choruses in detail. Furthermore, Nos. 3 and 6 had not yet been composed, and No 9 was an aria for tenor rather than the present duet. All scores which provide an English text credit the translation to Alfred Novello. There are, however, a number of differences between Breitkopf & Härtel's full score and Novello's vocal score, mostly of underlay, quite often of actual words, and the final chorus has a totally different text in the two scores. The Breitkopf & Härtel text to the final chorus runs as follows: 'O give thanks to the Lord, praise Him, all ye people. For He shall come to judge the earth with righteousness.' In this edition the words are printed as in the Novello vocal score which it replaces, major variants from the full score being given in footnotes. Thus, both the old and new Novello scores can be used together. Incidentally, it is interesting to note that Mendelssohn disliked the English title of the work, writing to his friend Karl Klingemann that he hoped the title would be 'Song of Praise' - 'Hymn - certainly not!'

SOURCES

A   Breitkopf & Härtel 1841, Full Score, German/English.
B   Breitkopf & Härtel 1875, Full Score, German, ed. Julius Rietz.
C   Eulenberg 1980, Study Score, German/English, ed. Roger Fiske.
D   Novello 1841, Vocal Score, English.
E   Novello 1857, Vocal Score, 8vo edition, German/English.
F   Novello c.1890, Full Score, English.
G   Novello c. 1910, Vocal Score, English, with an historical note by F G Edwards.

---

1   The text references have been researched by Annemarie Clostermann in her book: *Mendelssohn Bartholdys kirchenmusikalisches Schaffen. Neue Untersuchungen zu Geschichte, Form und Inhalt*, Mainz, 1989, S.111. It is clear that Mendelssohn made considerable changes to the texts used, and in some cases no source could be firmly identified.

2   Novello vocal score, c. 1910, English, with an historical note by F G Edwards

NOTES

No 2

b.113: In **B** and **C** note 2 in Horns 3 and 4 is also altered from d′ to c′ to fit the change made for the second violins

No 2a

A reads 'all my soul declare' for 'and my inmost soul' throughout this number.

b.6: **C** has a note: 'Chorus: English vocal scores have p on 4th beat, and perhaps full scores should too.' They do.

b.6: Soloist: **B**, **C** and **F** have 'Tutti' on beat 1 and 'Solo' on beat 4; **A** has neither, though it does give 'Tutti' and 'Solo' throughout the rest of the number when the chorus join in, as do all except **G**. **C** suggest that 'Tutti' 'implies that the soloist need not sing, 'Solo' that she must.' This gives a good reason for not marking a 'Tutti' in this bar.

No 3

b.7: **A** and **D** read 'cried', all others 'cry'; 'cried' is surely correct, matching 'sat' in bar 6, and see text of No 4.

b.8: **C** has a note: 'English vocal scores have impossible underlaying for the translation'; **E** certainly does, but all others have the rhythm and underlay as printed here, though **D** makes the first note a d″.

b.11: All except **D** and **G** complete the bar with a crotchet rest and pause.

No 4

b.7: Basses beat 4: b in **A** corrected in pencil to g in BL Hirsch iv 841, b in **C**, **D**, **E**, g in **B**, **F**, **G**.

No 5

A and **D** give 'Solo' and 'Tutti' throughout this number, other editions apply the terms inconsistently if at all.

No 6

bb.9-10, 44-45: **A** reads 'Hell in its terrors'.

bb.32-35, 67-70, 73-77: **A** reads 'I will be to thee-light'.

b.126: 'Pause' presumably indicates a break between the end of the tenor's pause note and the entry of the soprano.

No 7

b.27: **C** has a note: 'Alto note 3 g′ in previous editions, but it cannot be right'. The note is a′ in all editions except **E**. Soprano: from last quaver of bar 87 through bar 88 **A** reads 'the ar - mour of', with the same in the tenor a bar later; this matches the German. Soprano: **A** reads 'ar-' for the whole of bar 115 and the tied e″ of bar 116, with '-armour, let's' for the last two quavers; this matches the German.

No 8

C has a note: 'Some editions assume a mistake for crotchet = 84, but the marking at bar 16 shows that the quaver is right.' **D** and **E** give crotchet, but also give crotchet at bar 16; all other editions give quaver in both places. The text of this hymn by M. Rinkart (1586-1649) was translated by Catherine Winkworth (1827-1878) as the well known hymn, to the same chorale tune, 'Now thank we all our God'.

No 9

bb.1-2: and similar: **A** reads 'therefore thy mercy' for 'alway thy mercy'. **C** has a note: 'The underlay in English vocal scores has been corrected.' It is only wrong in **E**.

bb.9-12 and similar: **A** reads 'My tongue shall declare the blessings hourly bestowed by thee.'

b.9: 'speaks' in **A**, **B**, **F** and **G**, but 'speak' in **C**, **D** and **E**, which is grammatically correct.

bb.18-19: all Novello scores give 'ever thy praise'; **A** and **C** give 'singing thy praise', clearly correct.

b.21 and similar: **A** reads 'thickest' for 'foulest'.

b.57: soprano last note c″, **C**, **E**; tenor last note e′, **C**, **D**, and **E**.

b.62 (tenor) and 63 (soprano): sources inconsistent; sf in bar 62 in **B**, **C** and **F** only, in bar 63 in all but **A**, **B**, and **C**.

b.72 beat 2: Soprano has *sf* as well as *f* in **A**, **B** and **E**; tenor has *sf* as well as f in **D** and **E**.

bb.81-89: **A** reads 'I call'd upon thy name, O Lord' for 'yet call'd I on thy name, O God'.

★

This new edition of the *Hymn of Praise* follows the layout of the previous edition (catalogue number NOV070203) page for page, to allow this new edition to be used side-by-side with the edition it supersedes. The page numbering of this revised edition starts with page 1. The numbering of the previous edition (which started with page 23) is retained in small brackets in small type.

HYMN OF PRAISE

CANTATA

FELIX MENDELSSOHN

No. 2
Psalm cl, 6

Chorus: All men, all things

Allegro moderato, maestoso ♩ = 100

* Bass beat 4: rhythm ♩♪ B,C,E

* L.H. beat 4: rhythm ♪♩ in **B,C,E,F**

* RH note 3: d' altered to c' in **B,C,** and see Preface

* Tenor note 3: c' in **A,B,F** and **G,** given as d' in **C,D,E**

No. 2a
Psalm ciii, 1,2

Solo and Chorus: Praise thou the Lord*

* see Preface † *sf* given only in **A**

great lov-ing kind - ness. Praise thou the Lord, O my spi - rit, and___ for-get thou

not, and for-get thou not, for-get thou not all His ben - e-fits, Praise thou the

Praise thou the

Praise thou the

Praise thou the

Praise thou the

16 (38)

No. 3

Recitative and Air: Sing ye praise

Psalm cvii 2, 10

Allegro moderato ♩ = 80

* see Preface

* RH note 7: c" for a' in **D, E, G**   † voice: **_p_** in **B, C, F, G**

* voice note 2: **p** in **B,C,F,G**

No.4   *Chorus:* All ye that cried unto the Lord

No. 5   *Duet and Chorus:* I waited for the Lord

Psalm x1, 1,4

A
Lord.
SOPRANO SOLO 2
I
A Chorus
SOPRANO
O blessed are they that hope and trust in the Lord.
ALTO
O blessed are they that hope and trust in the Lord.
TENOR
O blessed are they that hope and trust in the Lord.
BASS
O blessed are they that hope and trust in the Lord.
I wait - ed for the Lord, He in - cli - ned un - to me, and He heard my com-plaint. I wait - ed for the
wait - ed for the Lord, He in - cli - ned un - to me, He heard my com- - plaint, He heard my com-plaint. I wait - ed for the Lord, He in -

* see Preface

* Chorus beat 2: *fz* in **A**, *sf* missing in **E,G**   † Soprano 1 and 2: *f* missing in **A,B**

*all voices: ♩♫ in **A**
hope,— O

No.6

Solo: The sorrows of death

Psalm cxvi, 3
Ephesians v, 14
Isaiah xxi, 11-12

TENOR SOLO

The sor - rows of death had clo - sed all a-round me, and Hell's dark ter - rors had got hold up-

-on me, with trou - ble and deep hea - vi - ness, with trou - ble and deep

hea - vi - ness; but, said the Lord, "Come, a - rise,

come, a - rise_____ from the dead, and a-wake, thou that sleep - est, and a-

* see Preface

-wake, thou that sleep-est, I bring thee sal-va-tion."

The sor-rows of death had clo-sed all a-round me, and Hell's dark ter-rors had got hold up-on me, with trou-ble and deep hea-vi-ness, with trou-ble and deep hea-vi-ness; but, said the Lord, "Come, a-rise, come, a-

A

*see Preface

* **_p_ in C,D,E,G**

* no *cresc.* in **C,D,E**   † no mm. in **A,B,C**   ** voice and piano: no *sf* in **A,D**

* see Preface

No. 7
Romans xiii, 12

Chorus: The night is departing

* see Preface

* soprano: no *cresc.* in A

* see Preface † Bass bars 98-107: no *sf*'s in **A,B**

* see Preface

* attacca in A only

attacca*

No. 8   *Chorale:* Let all men men praise the Lord

* see Preface
† 2nd Tenor note 2: b in **C,D,E**

* **C** gives 'tri-une' for 'Three-One' without comment, but a good suggestion.

No. 9   *Duet:* My song shall be alway Thy mercy*

* see Preface

* bars 54,55 tenor note 1: > given in **B,C,F,G** † see Preface

* see Preface   † Soprano note 5: no *sf*, **C,D,E**

No. 10   Chorus: Ye nations, offer to the Lord*

Psalm xcvi, 7

* see Preface

* no ‾<‾ in **A**

* Soprano, Alto, Tenor entries bb.143-5: no *sf* in **C,D,E**

* Underlay: ♩ ♩ ♩ in **C** (and in German)

* Soprano note 1: d" in **C, E**